In loving memory of Stanley, who always encouraged me.

To my beloved children, who are fulfilling their Jewish dreams and mine:
Claire and Larry, Jonathan, Beth and Jeff.

To my adoring grandchildren, who are learning to love Torah and who light up my life:
Shoshana, Gabi, Sammie, Ari, Brett Aaron, Samuel, Shira, Seth, and Sarah.

To all children everywhere with hope for peace.

— MARVELL GINSBURG

In loving memory of my mother, Gusta, and my father, Tovia, who survived the Holocaust,
and in loving memory of my grandparents, aunts, uncles, and cousins who didn't.
May their memory be a blessing.

To my amazing grandchildren, Jason, William, Andrew, Oliver,
Jeffrey, Hannah, Abigail, and Zoja — the fourth generation.

— MARTIN LEMELMAN

A portion of the proceeds from the sales of this book will go to support further educational resources to promote empathy and understanding among all people.

The Kopin family would like to thank Cottage Door Press for their gracious contributions in shepherding this new edition of *The Tattooed Torah* through its beautiful redesign and publication.

First published in the United States in 1983.
Second edition published in the United States in 1994.

Published by Cottage Door Press, LLC
5005 Newport Drive, Rolling Meadows, Illinois 60008

978-1-64638-551-5

www.cottagedoorpress.com

Cottage Door Press® and the Cottage Door Press® logo
are registered trademarks of Cottage Door Press, LLC.

the Tattooed Torah

 cottage door press

WRITTEN BY **Marvell Ginsburg**

ILLUSTRATED BY **Martin Lemelman**

This is the story of a little tattooed *Torah*. It was always little but not always tattooed.

Many, many years ago, before you were born, Little Torah lived in a handsome wooden *aron kodesh* (ark) that had an embroidered velvet *parochet* (curtain).

Next to Little Torah in the aron kodesh stood several big Torahs, wearing soft velvet mantles of scarlet, purple, and blue. Some big Torahs had silver crowns. Little Torah thought they looked like kings and queens. Other big Torahs had silver bells that made a gentle jingling sound when the Torahs were taken out of the ark on *Shabbat* mornings and other holidays.

Oh, how sweetly the bells chimed when the grown-ups hugged the Torahs lovingly in their arms and marched with them through the synagogue!

Every *Bar Mitzvah* wanted to carry Little Torah in the procession and read his Torah portion from it. Shabbat after Shabbat, holiday after holiday, year after year, Little Torah was held by a child marching in the procession.

Little Torah was very proud.

One day everything changed.

Little Torah heard a different kind of marching sound. It was not the sound of Jewish people marching into synagogue to pray. It was not the sound of people marching in the Torah service procession, singing Hebrew songs. It was loud, mean marching with loud, mean talk.

An evil man, Adolf Hitler, had started a war. His Nazi soldiers marched into Brno, Czechoslovakia, Little Torah's city. The Nazis closed all the synagogues. They ordered that all the Torahs, mantles, and other religious items be sent to the city of Prague.

Little Torah was thrown on a pile of Torahs
in the back of a dark truck.

As the truck rumbled out of the town, Little Torah asked
tearfully, "How could such a terrible thing happen to Torahs?"

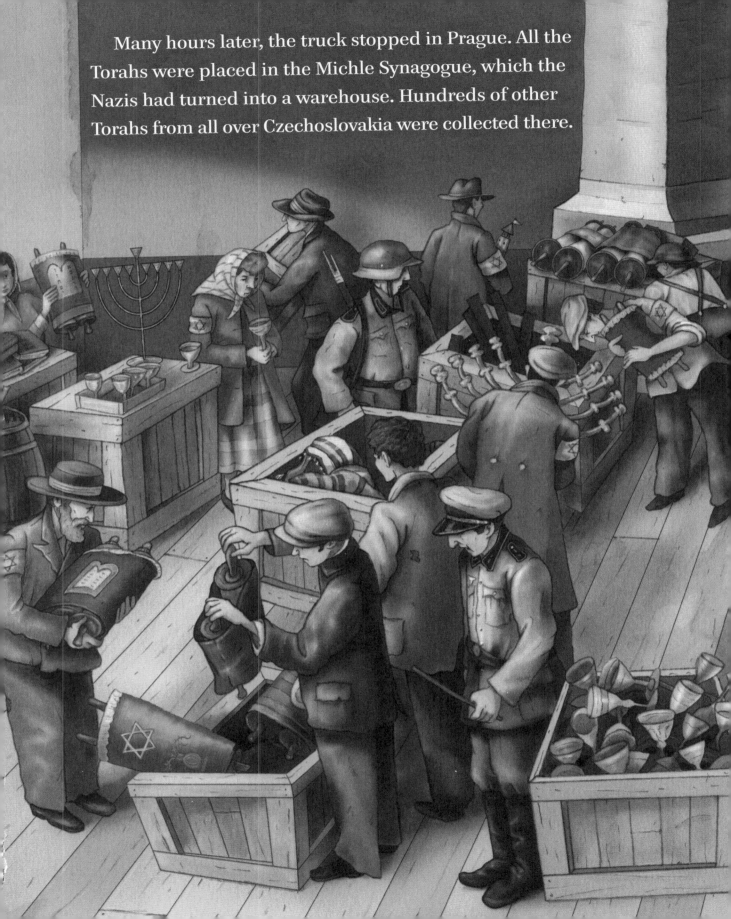

Many hours later, the truck stopped in Prague. All the Torahs were placed in the Michle Synagogue, which the Nazis had turned into a warehouse. Hundreds of other Torahs from all over Czechoslovakia were collected there.

The Nazis forced workers to tattoo a number on each Torah.
Then, in a book, they wrote the number of the Torah and the
place from which it came.

Little Torah was angry. "They have no right to tattoo a Torah!
A Torah is the most precious possession of the Jewish people."

Just then, a Nazi soldier grabbed Little Torah. He ordered a worker to paint a number on the bottom of one of its wooden rollers and attach a tag to the other. Then Little Torah was put on a rough wooden shelf.

Every day Little Torah saw Nazi soldiers march into the warehouse and deliver truckloads of Torahs. The workers added more tattoos, more tags, more numbers in the record book.

One day the marching stopped. The war was over. The Nazis were gone. But Little Torah and all the other Torahs remained in the warehouse. They lay on the damp, dusty, dirty shelves for many years until they were rescued and sent in sealed railroad cars to a synagogue in London, England.

Many years later in America, a little Jewish boy came home from religious school and said to his father, "Daddy, I can't lift the Torah at services; it's too heavy for me!" Arthur Weil, his daddy, answered, "Oh, Tommy, I'm so glad you told me. That gives me an idea. Now I know what to give your school for a *tzedakah* gift. I will look for a small child-sized Torah."

Mr. Weil asked many people where he could find a small Torah. Someone told him that Torahs were available from the Westminster Synagogue in London. He flew there and met Mrs. Ruth Shaffer, who was in charge of the Torahs.

She led Mr. Weil into a big storeroom. There in front of him were more than fifteen hundred Torahs on wooden racks. One was wrapped in a tattered *tallit*. Another was tied with a child's belt. Many were damaged because they had not been unrolled for over twenty years.

Mr. Weil couldn't believe his eyes. "Where did you get all these Torahs?" he asked.

Mrs. Shaffer told him what the Nazis had done. Mr. Weil went closer to look at the Torahs. He saw the numbers on the bottom of their rollers.

"How could anyone do this to Torahs?" he asked. Tears rolled down his cheeks. He stood there crying for a long time. "Torahs don't belong in a warehouse," he said. "They belong in synagogues. They need to be used and studied."

"That's just what we do," said Mrs. Shaffer. "The Westminster Synagogue sends these Torahs to Jewish congregations all over the world."

Mr. Weil looked around the storeroom and stopped when he saw Little Torah. He took it down from the shelf and saw the number 32804 tattooed on its roller. In the record book he discovered that Little Torah had come from Brno. Holding Little Torah in his arms, Mr. Weil knew that his son and other children in his religious school would be able to carry Little Torah.

Mr. Weil wrapped the little scroll in brown paper to protect it. After boarding the plane in London, Mr. Weil buckled Little Torah into the seat next to his. "From now on, Little Torah, we will always take good care of you," he promised. Little Torah was happy now. Soon it would be in the arms of a Jewish child.

Back home, Mr. Weil had a red velvet mantle made especially to fit Little Torah. The mantle was decorated with a gold Jewish star and the word *Zachor* (Remember). How handsome Little Torah felt inside its new mantle and aron kodesh!

The school principal invited all the children, their parents, grandparents, and teachers to a special service in honor of their new Torah.

Little Torah shivered with excitement as it was taken from the ark and carried in a procession. Little Torah was handed to the youngest child, who led them in a joyous march around the building, singing, *"Torah, Torah, Torah, Torah, Torah, Torah, Torah tzivah lanu Moshe."* (The Torah was commanded to us by Moses.)

When the procession returned to the sanctuary, Little Torah was unrolled, and two children read the portion of the week.

At the end of the service, Little Torah was placed in the aron kodesh. Mr. Weil then told everyone the story of the tattooed Torah. Listening from its new home, Little Torah sighed with happiness.

"And now, children," Mr. Weil concluded, "the little tattooed Torah is yours. May it dwell forever in this house of love and learning!"

All the children and grown-ups softly said, "*Amen*."

To My Reader

A mother participating in a discussion on how to deal with the *Shoah* (Holocaust) with her young children related the following: "My parents are survivors, but they could never talk about their experiences." Other parents nodded sympathetically and joined in. "I feel overwhelmed and don't know where or how to begin or at what age. I don't want my children to feel like it's bad to be Jewish. I can't understand the Holocaust myself. How can I teach it to my children?"

The foregoing concerns are fairly typical of comments made by parents on this subject. Yet even though the theme of our Jewish history for thousands of years has been "bad kings who wanted to make Jews stop being Jews," we have always had happy endings.

Happy endings reassure us and give us a sense of mastery so we feel okay. We have been around for thousands of years. Hitler and his Nazis are gone. We remain. Young children hear and notice things. They ask questions. They deserve answers they can understand at their levels, as they try to determine who they are and what kind of world this is.

Very young children know about death and grief. Pets and plants die. A friend moves away. They experience the loss of a family member or friend. When "tough topics" are introduced gradually to the young, in an honest, appropriate manner by loving, supportive adults, children can handle them and grow into a deeper understanding as they mature.

The writer has read *The Tattooed Torah* to many groups from ages four and up.
Here are some of their comments:

"If I was there I would punch those Nazis in the mouth."

"I think the Torah was really a child. I know people slept on hard shelves."

"Why did the Nazis bother us? We're just people like everybody else!"

"I can't wait 'til I read from the Torah."

"I take that book with me to Temple every Shabbat."

Here is an example of what a parent can say to their questioning four-year-old:

"A very long time ago something happened to Bubby and Zayde and many other Jewish people in Germany and other countries very far away. Very mean Nazi soldiers took them away from their homes to places called concentration camps. The Nazis were ordered to do this by their very evil leader, Hitler. They made them work too hard. Many people died. Bubby doesn't like to think about that. It upsets her. She and Zayde feel safe now. There are no more Nazis. Hitler is dead. We work hard to make sure everyone is safe and can live the kind of life they want whether they are Jews, Christians, Muslims, or any other people of faith."

We will always remember what happened. We won't let it happen again. We lay the foundation for teaching about the Holocaust by conveying our own positive sense of Jewishness, by ongoing celebrations of Jewish life, and by our expectation that we will be around for years to come. Then the answers we give our children will be accepted, absorbed, and integrated positively into their *neshamas*.

Marvell Ginsburg

Glossary

Amen *(ah-men)*
A word used to express agreement, spoken aloud by a group of people at the conclusion of a prayer.

Aron Kodesh *(ah-rone koh-desh)*
A special cabinet, or ark, in Jewish houses of worship (synagogues) used for storing Torah scrolls.

Bar/Bat Mitzvah *(bar mitz-vah/baht mitz-vah)*
The religious life-cycle event celebrating a Jewish boy's (*bar*) or girl's (*bat*) coming of age. According to Jewish law, Jewish children are ready by age thirteen to take on Jewish responsibilities, like reading Hebrew (the ancient language of the Jewish people) and participating in public worship by chanting passages from the Torah in a synagogue.

Neshama *(neh-shah-mah)*
The Hebrew word for "soul."

Parochet *(pah-row-het)*
An ornate, fancy curtain covering the opening of the aron kodesh.

Shabbat *(shah-baht)*
The Hebrew word for "Sabbath," the Jewish observance of the day of rest, occurring weekly from sunset on Friday night until sunset on Saturday night.

Shoah *(show-ah)*

The Holocaust (deriving from the Greek word meaning "sacrifice by fire"), or the Shoah (the Hebrew word meaning "catastrophe"), refers to the destruction of the European Jewish population by Nazi Germany and its allies during World War II.

Tallit *(tah-leet)*

A prayer shawl with fringes, worn by religious Jews while praying, symbolizing the Jewish people's commitment to Torah and Jewish law.

Torah *(toe-rah)*

The Jewish people's sacred collection of laws and stories, handwritten on a parchment scroll, also known as the Five Books of Moses.

Tzedakah *(tse-dah-kah)*

The Hebrew word for "righteousness," most commonly used to mean giving charity, considered to be an ethical obligation of the Jewish people.

Zachor *(zah-hor)*

The Hebrew word for "remember" — a central concept in Holocaust education, empowering every Jew to keep the stories of the Holocaust alive from generation to generation.

Art Weil holding Little Torah alongside Tommy Weil (age 8) and family during the installation ceremony at Solomon Schechter Day School, 1972, Chicago, IL

Solomon Schechter Day School student (age 8) holding Little Torah, 20

Marvell Ginsburg (author) with her grandson Brett Kopin (age 8) holding Little Torah, 1998

Little Torah inside the ark at Solomon Schechter Day School

Teacher chanting from Little Torah to the second-grade class at Solomon Schechter Day School

Brno, Czechoslovakia— Little Torah's hometown before the Holocaust

Little Torah with red velvet mantle

Little Torah from Brno, Czechoslovakia, with #32804 painted on the roller

Michle Church, Prague (former synagogue), where Little Torah was stored during the Holocaust

Westminster Synagogue, London, England, where Torahs from Prague were sent after the Holocaust

The remaining Torah scrolls at the Memorial Scrolls Trust Museum, Westminster Synagogue, London, England